50 Sensational Stir-fries

STEP-BY-STEP
50 Sensational Stir-fries

Liz Trigg

Photography by Michelle Garrett

HERMES
HOUSE

This edition published by Hermes House
an imprint of
Anness Publishing Limited
Hermes House
88-89 Blackfriars Road
London SE1 8HA

Published in the USA by Hermes House
Anness Publishing Inc., 27 West 20th Street, New York, NY 10011;
(800) 354-9657

A CIP catalogue record for this book is available from the British Library

ISBN 1 84038 442 5

Publisher: Joanna Lorenz
Project Editor: Lindsay Porter
Designer : Peter Laws
Jacket Designer : Peter Butler
Photographer and Stylist : Michelle Garrett

Printed and bound in Hong Kong

© Anness Publishing Limited 1999

1 3 5 7 9 10 8 6 4 2

CONTENTS

INTRODUCTION

Stir-frying is an ancient cooking technique that originated in the Far East, but its popularity has spread throughout the world. It is an ideal technique for the modern cook: dishes can be stir-fried in a matter of minutes, using very little oil, which means the ingredients lose little of their nutritional value, and are relatively low in fat.

Many of the recipes in this book are Oriental favourites, originating from all over the Far East, but traditional Western dishes have been adapted to take advantage of this quick technique – you'll find recipes for Beef Sukiyaki and Duck and Ginger Chop Suey, Chicken Liver Stir-fry and stir-fried Turkey with Sage. Don't be afraid to try the recipes if you haven't got a wok – a large frying pan with a heavy base will work just as well, although you may find in some cases it is necessary to cook the ingredients in smaller batches.

Once you begin, you'll be amazed at the versatility of the technique, and may find you can adapt some of your own favourites. Whether you want a spicy starter or a sizzling dessert, consider stir-frying for a quick, healthy and delicious dish.

Equipment

You will find most of the cooking equipment you have around the kitchen will produce good results. As mentioned previously, it isn't even essential to use a wok. However, if you would like to invest in some good kitchen equipment, or wish to use the authentic tools of the trade, the following may be of interest:

Bamboo skewers
These are widely used for barbecues and grilled foods. They are discarded after use.

Chopping board
A good quality chopping board with a thick surface will last for years.

Chopping knife
If you are not comfortable using a cleaver, a large, heavy chopping knife can be used.

Citrus zester
This tool is designed to remove the zest while leaving the bitter white pith. It can also be used for shaving fresh coconut.

Cleaver
The weight of the cleaver makes it ideal for chopping all kinds of ingredients. Keep this as sharp as possible.

Cooking chopsticks
These are extra-long, and allow you to stir ingredients in the wok, while keeping a safe distance.

Draining wire
This is designed to sit on the side of the wok, and is used mainly for deep-frying.

Food processor
This is a quick alternative to the pestle and mortar.

Ladle
A long-handled ladle is very useful for spooning out soup, stock or sauces.

Pestle and mortar
This is useful for grinding small amounts of spices.

Rice paddle
This is used to fluff up rice after cooking.

Saucepan
A good saucepan with a tight-fitting lid is essential for cooking rice properly. It may also be used for stir-frying.

Sharpening stone
A traditional tool for sharpening knives and cleavers, available from hardware stores.

Stainless steel skimmer
This can be used when strong flavours are likely to affect bare metal cooking implements.

Wire skimmer
This is used to remove cooked food from boiling water or hot fat. It should not be used with fish-based liquids as the strong flavour is likely to affect the metal.

Wok
The shape of the wok allows ingredients to be cooked in a minimum of fat, thus retaining freshness and flavour. There are several varieties available including the carbon steel round-bottomed wok or Pau wok. This wok is best suited to a gas hob, where you will be able to control the amount of heat needed more easily. The carbon steel flat-bottomed wok is best for use on electric or solid fuel hobs, as it will give a better distribution of heat. A small round-bottomed wok enables you to prepare small quantities quickly, as it takes less time to heat up.

wok

cooking chopsticks

stainless steel skimmers

food processor

bamboo skewers

saucepan

chopping board

chopping
knife

draining
wire

sharpening
stone

citrus
zester

cleavers

pestle and
mortar

rice paddle

wire skimmer

Fresh Produce

Almost any ingredient can be stir-fried, and, as the freshness and flavour of the produce will not be affected by cooking, it is important to choose the freshest, best quality ingredients you can.

Baby sweetcorn
These may be stir-fried whole or chopped.

Beansprouts
These impart a lovely texture to vegetable and meat dishes. Do not keep for longer than a few days before using or they will brown and wilt.

Chinese lettuce
The crispy leaves are ideal for stir-frying. Shred or chop finely before using.

Coconut
Fresh coconut is infinitely better tasting than any other coconut product available. When selecting a coconut, choose one with plenty of milk inside.

Cucumber
Cucumber can be chopped and sliced finely and stir-fried, or used in relishes to accompany main dishes.

Fennel
Slice and stir-fry to impart an aniseed flavour.

Garlic
Crush or chop finely.

Leeks
Slice into very thin rings before stir-frying.

Lemons
Use the grated rind and juice in stir-fries and marinades, and lemon slices as a garnish.

Limes
Use the grated rind and juice in stir-fries and marinades, and lime slices as a garnish.

Lychees
Peel to use, remove the stone, and halve or slice.

Mango
Ripe mango should have a slightly soft flesh. Peel and remove the stone before use.

Mooli
This has a very subtle flavour.

Mustard and cress
This is usually added at the last moment, or as a garnish.

Onions
Every variety of onion makes a tasty addition to stir-fries.

Oyster mushrooms
Use as ordinary mushrooms,

wiping clean with a damp cloth or paper towel.

Patty pan squash
These small squash have a taste similar to marrow.

Peppers
Deseed and chop into strips before stir-frying.

Radishes
Slice finely, or use tiny baby radishes as a garnish.

Shitake mushrooms
These tasty, firm-textured mushrooms may be treated as ordinary mushrooms. Only use half the amount if using the dried variety. Soak in boiling water for 20 minutes, and save the soaking water for a sauce.

Spinach
Remove the stalks before using and wash thoroughly in several changes of cold water to remove any grit.

Spring onions
Chop finely before using, or cut into julienne strips.

Anti-clockwise from top left: *red peppers, coconut, lychees, shitake mushrooms, spinach, onions, beansprouts, mustard and cress, Chinese lettuce, cucumber, mooli, radish, baby sweetcorn, spring onions, leeks, oyster and shitake mushrooms, yellow pepper, fennel, celery.* In centre basket, from top left: *patty pan squash, mango, limes, garlic, lemons.*

Herbs and Spices

The following can be used to enhance fresh ingredients. Whenever possible, use fresh herbs for the best flavour. If using dried herbs you will need smaller amounts as the flavour is less subtle. Some of the flavourings used in this book include the following:

Chillies
Generally, the smallest chillies are the hottest. Removing the seeds will reduce the heat. Chop finely, and stir-fry with oil. Always work in a well-ventilated area and do not allow chillies to come into contact with your skin or eyes.

Chilli powder
Many varieties of dried chilli powder are now available, each varying in strength.

Chinese chives
These have a mild flavour similar to a Spanish onion. They should be cooked very lightly and are wonderful served raw as a garnish.

Coriander leaves
Fresh coriander imparts a unique, refreshing taste and aroma. Bunches of fresh leaves can be kept for up to 5 days in a jar of water.

Coriander seeds
Whole seeds can be dry-fried (without oil) with other ingredients and are also available ground.

Cumin
Cumin is generally dry-fried and combines well with coriander seeds. It is widely used in beef dishes.

Galingale
This is sometimes known as Lengkuas. This root has a mingled flavour of pine and citrus. It may be peeled and treated in the same way as root ginger. It is available from Oriental stores.

Lemon grass
This aromatic herb has a thin tapering stem and a citrusy, verbena flavour. To use, thinly slice the bulb end of the root.

Lime leaves
These are often called kaffir lime leaves. They are excellent in marinades, and often need to be bruised to release the flavour.

Paprika
Paprika is made from a variety of sweet red pepper. It is mild in flavour, and adds colour. Add to stir-fries or sprinkle on finished dishes.

Parsley
Parsley, both curly and flat-leaf, is an ideal and attractive garnish. Flat-leaf parsley has a stronger flavour than the curly variety.

Root ginger
Peel off the skin of the fresh root and use sliced, chopped or grated. Always buy the root with the smoothest skin as it is the freshest. The flesh should be a creamy colour, and not too yellow.

Rosemary
This is usually added to lamb and pork dishes. It has a strong flavour.

Star anise
This spice has a pungent, aniseed-like taste. It can either be ground, or used whole in marinades.

Turmeric
Turmeric is used for its attractive yellow colouring. It has a slightly musty taste and aroma.

Right: *Flavour enhancers for stir-fries might include herbs such as parsley, rosemary, or coriander, or spices such as chilli powder, cumin, paprika, turmeric, ginger or star anise. Lemon grass, lime leaves, galingale or fresh chillies will add a distinctly eastern flavour.*

Store Cupboard Ingredients

The following ingredients can be used to create authentic tasting Eastern stir-fries. They can be purchased in most large supermarkets or Oriental food stores.

Creamed coconut
This is available in a solid block form from Oriental food stores and large supermarkets and is ideal for giving an intense coconut flavour. Simply add water to make a thick coconut paste. The paste may be thinned with more water until the correct consistency and flavour is acquired.

Extra-virgin olive oil
This is the highest grade olive oil and has a very intense flavour. Do not use this oil for cooking, but drizzle it over the finished dish before serving.

Grapeseed oil
A lightly flavoured oil, good for stir-frying delicately flavoured foods.

Hoisin sauce
This is often called barbecue sauce, and is a spicy/smoky condiment with a distinctive smoky flavour.

Olive oil
The characteristic flavour of olive oil is not suitable for Oriental stir-fries. Use when you want to impart a Mediterranean flavour.

Oyster sauce
Made from oyster extract, this speciality sauce is used in many fish dishes, soups and sauces.

Peanut butter
This can be used in Indonesian satay dishes. It makes a good sauce when heated. Use varieties without sugar for the best flavour.

Red chilli sauce
A sweet, hot sauce that is often used to flavour home-made sauces, or used on its own as a dip.

Red wine vinegar
Use this vinegar for sauces, dressings and marinades for a robust flavour.

Sake (rice wine)
Sake is used mainly in Japanese stir-fries. The best grades are used for drinking, and the lower grades for sauces and marinades, and also for dressings.

Sesame oil
This is used more as a flavouring than for cooking. It is very intensely flavoured, so only a few drops will be needed at a time.

Sherry vinegar
Use for sauces and marinades for a strong flavour.

Soy sauce
Dark soy sauce is sweet and thick, and the best variety is made from naturally fermented soy. Light soy sauce is a less intense version of the classic dark soy sauce.

Sugar
Both white caster sugar and soft brown sugar are used in marinades and sauces.

Sunflower oil
A good all-purpose cooking oil with a mild flavour.

Teriyaki sauce
Use in barbecued and stir-fried dishes, and as a marinade for meat or fish.

White wine vinegar
Use for sauces, marinades and dressings.

sesame oil

olive oil

creamed coconut

brown sugar

white wine vinegar

sake (rice wine)

extra-virgin olive oil

sherry vinegar

grapeseed oil

sunflower oil

red wine vinegar

peanut butter

light soy sauce

oyster sauce

dark soy sauce

teriyaki sauce

hoisin sauce

sugar

General Rules for Stir-frying

Stir-frying takes very little actual cooking time, often no more than a matter of minutes. For this reason it is important that all the ingredients are prepared ahead of time — washed, peeled or grated as required, and cut to approximately the same shape and size, to ensure even cooking.

1 Always heat the wok (or frying pan, if using) for a few minutes before adding the oil or any other ingredients.

2 If adding oil, swirl the oil into the wok and allow it to heat up before adding the next ingredients.

3 When adding the first ingredients, reduce the heat a little. This will ensure they are not overcooked or burnt by the time the remaining ingredients have been added to the wok.

4 Once all the ingredients have been added, quickly increase the heat, as this will allow the dish to cook in the least possible time. This allows the ingredients to retain a crisp, fresh texture, and prevents them from becoming soggy or laden with oil.

5 Use a long handled scoop or spatula to turn the ingredients as you stir-fry. This will allow the ingredients to cook evenly and quickly.

6 It may be easier to slice meat for stir-frying if it has been frozen slightly for an hour or so. By the time you have sliced it, the meat will be thawed to cook.

Seasoning your Wok

If you are using a new wok or frying pan you will need to prepare it as follows to ensure the best results:

1 Heat the wok or frying pan with 30–45 ml/2–3 tbsp salt for about 15 minutes. Wipe out the salt and continue to use as recommended.

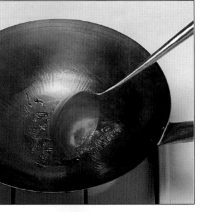

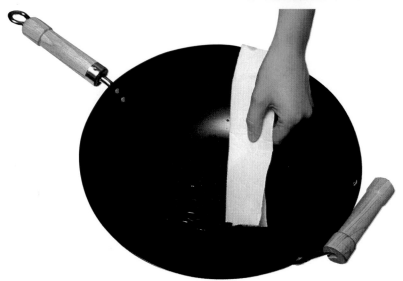

2 To clean your wok, wipe out the inside with kitchen towels, where possible, keeping washing with detergent to a minimum. A naturally seasoned pan will create a good non-stick surface.

Preparing Spring Onions

Spring onions can be used in stir-fries to flavour oil, as vegetables in their own right, or as decoration.

1 Trim off the root with a sharp knife.

2 For an intense flavour, cut into matchsticks and stir-fry with vegetables of the same size.

3 Slice thinly to stir-fry with crushed garlic to flavour the cooking oil.

Preparing Chillies

The strong flavour of chilli is wonderful in cooking, but fresh chillies must be handled with care. Always work in a well ventilated area, and do not let the chilli touch your skin. Do not rub your eyes after handling.

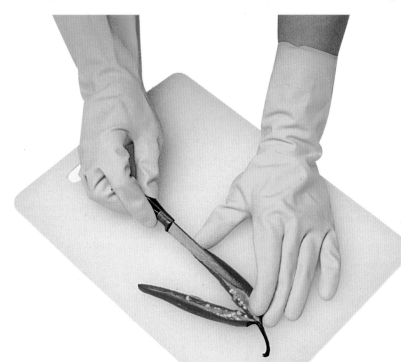

 Slice the chillies, and remove the seeds. You may want to wear rubber gloves to protect your skin.

2 Finely chop and use as required.

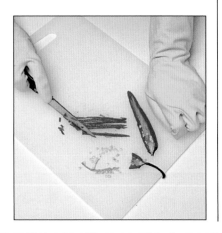

Shredding Cabbage

Delicious stir-fried, this method means the cabbage will cook evenly.

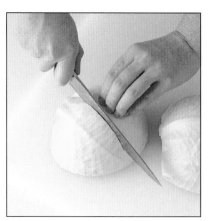 

1 Use a large knife to cut the cabbage into quarters.

2 Cut the core from each quarter.

3 Slice across each quarter to form fine shreds.

Preparing Coconut Flakes

Although many convenient coconut products are available – canned milk, creamed coconut, desiccated coconut flakes – nothing beats fresh coconut for flavour in cooking.

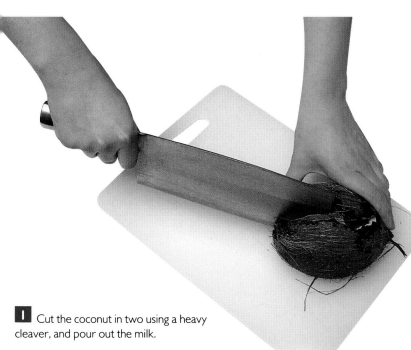

1 Cut the coconut in two using a heavy cleaver, and pour out the milk.

2 Peel the flesh away from the shell using a vegetable peeler.

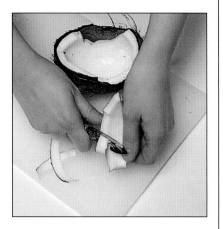

Preparing Ginger

Fresh root ginger is used in many Oriental stir-fries. Prepare as follows:

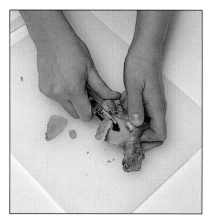
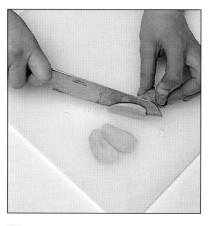

1 Peel the skin off the root. The skin should be smooth and blemish free (the smoother the skin, the fresher the ginger will be).

2 Cut the ginger into thin slices, using a sharp knife.

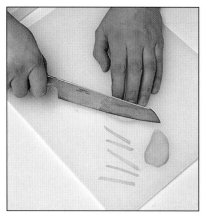

3 To stir-fry with spring onions or other vegetables, cut into julienne strips.

4 If adding to oil at the beginning of a recipe, as a flavouring, chop finely.

Slicing Onions

Stir-fry onion slices with the main vegetables. Ensure they are all cut to the same size for even cooking.

1 Peel the onion. Cut in half with a large knife and set it cut-side down on to a chopping board.

2 Cut out a triangular piece of the core from each half.

3 Cut across each half in vertical slices.

Chopping Onions

Diced onions can be used to flavour oil before stir-frying the main ingredients.

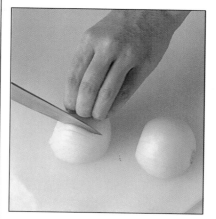

1 Peel the onion. Cut in half with a knife and set it cut-side down on a board. Make lengthwise vertical cuts along the onion, cutting almost through to the root.

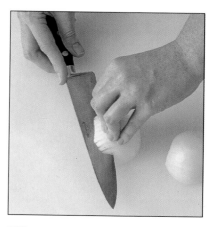

2 Make 2 horizontal cuts from the stalk and towards the root, but not through it.

3 Cut the onion crosswise to form small dice.

Preparing Mooli

This giant white radish is appreciated in stir-fries for its crisp texture.

1 Peel the mooli and cut into 7.5 cm/ 3 in length matchsticks for stir-frying.

2 To use as a relish, grate with a lemon zester. If you don't have a zester, chop the mooli very finely.

Cutting Julienne Strips

Small julienne strips of vegetables can be tied in individual bundles after cooking.

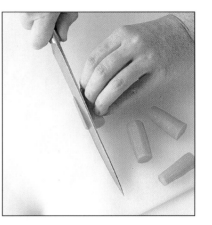 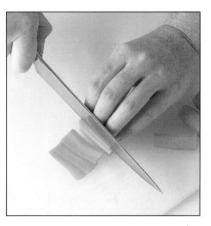

1 Peel the vegetable and use a large knife to cut it into 5 cm/2 in lengths. Cut a thin sliver from one side of the first piece so that it sits flat on the board.

2 Cut each strip into thin edges lengthwise on the board.

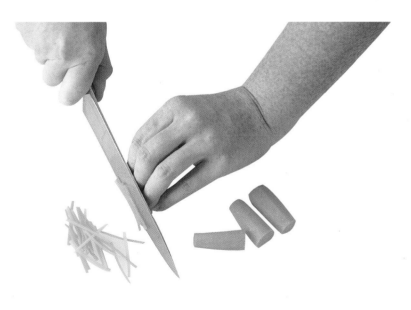

3 Stack the slices and cut through them to make fine strips.

Mini Spring Rolls

Eat these light crispy parcels with your fingers. If you like slightly spicier food, sprinkle them with a little cayenne pepper before serving.

Makes 20

INGREDIENTS
1 green chilli
125 ml/4 fl oz/½ cup vegetable oil
1 small onion, finely chopped
1 clove garlic, crushed
75 g/3 oz cooked chicken breast
1 small carrot, cut into fine
    matchsticks
1 spring onion, finely sliced
1 small red pepper, seeded and cut
    into fine matchsticks
25 g/1 oz beansprouts
5 ml/1 tsp sesame oil
4 large sheets filo pastry
1 × size 4 egg white, lightly beaten
long chives, to garnish (optional)
45 ml/3 tbsp light soy sauce, to serve

spring onions

chilli

pepper

garlic

beansprouts

COOK'S TIP

Be careful to avoid touching your face or eyes when deseeding and chopping chillies because they are very potent and may cause burning and irritation to the skin. Try preparing chillies under running water.

1 Carefully remove the seeds from the chilli and chop finely, wearing rubber gloves to protect your hands, if necessary.

2 Heat the wok, then add 30 ml/2 tbsp of the vegetable oil. When hot, add the onion, garlic and chilli. Stir-fry for 1 minute.

3 Slice the chicken thinly, then add to the wok and fry over a high heat, stirring constantly until browned.

4 Add the carrot, spring onion and red pepper and stir-fry for 2 minutes. Add the beansprouts, stir in the sesame oil and leave to cool.

COOK'S TIP

Always keep filo pastry sheets covered with a dry, clean cloth until needed, to prevent them drying out.

5 Cut each sheet of filo into 5 short strips. Place a small amount of filling at one end of each strip, then fold in the long sides and roll up the pastry. Seal and glaze the parcels with the egg white, then chill uncovered for 15 minutes before frying.

6 Wipe out the wok with kitchen towels, heat it, and add the remaining vegetable oil. When the oil is hot, fry the rolls in batches until crisp and golden brown. Drain on kitchen towels and serve dipped in light soy sauce.

Sesame Seed Chicken Bites

Best served warm, these crunchy bites are delicious accompanied by a glass of chilled dry white wine.

Makes 20

INGREDIENTS
175 g/6 oz raw chicken breast
2 cloves garlic, crushed
2.5 cm/1 in piece root ginger, peeled
   and grated
1 × size 4 egg white
5 ml/1 tsp cornflour
25 g/1 oz/¼ cup shelled pistachios,
   roughly chopped
60 ml/4 tbsp sesame seeds
30 ml/2 tbsp grapeseed oil
salt and freshly ground black pepper

FOR THE SAUCE
45 ml/3 tbsp/¼ cup hoisin sauce
15 ml/1 tbsp sweet chilli sauce

TO GARNISH
root ginger, finely shredded
pistachios, roughly chopped
fresh dill sprigs

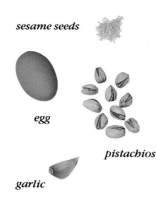

sesame seeds

egg

pistachios

garlic

ginger

1 Place the chicken, garlic, grated ginger, egg white and cornflour into the food processor and process them to a smooth paste.

2 Stir in the pistachios and season well with salt and pepper.

3 Roll into 20 balls and coat with sesame seeds. Heat the wok and add the oil. When the oil is hot, stir-fry the chicken bites in batches, turning regularly until golden. Drain on kitchen towels.

4 Make the sauce by mixing together the hoisin and chilli sauces in a bowl. Garnish the bites with shredded ginger, pistachios and dill, then serve hot, with a dish of sauce for dipping.

Mixed Spiced Nuts

These make an excellent accompaniment to drinks. They will store for up to a month in an air-tight container if they are not mixed together.

Serves 4–6

INGREDIENTS
75 g/3 oz dried unsweetened
 coconut flakes
75 ml/5 tbsp peanut oil
2.5 ml/½ tsp chilli powder
5 ml/1 tsp ground paprika
5 ml/1 tsp tomato purée
225 g/8 oz/2 cups unsalted cashews
225 g/8 oz/2 cups whole blanched
 almonds
60 ml/4 tbsp caster sugar
5 ml/1 tsp ground cumin
2.5 ml/½ tsp salt
freshly ground black pepper
mustard and cress, to garnish

cashews

paprika   *chilli powder*

cumin

almonds

1 Heat the wok, add the coconut flakes and dry-fry until golden. Leave to cool.

2 Heat the wok and add 45 ml/3 tbsp of the peanut oil. When the oil is hot, add the chilli, paprika and tomato purée. Gently stir-fry the cashews in the spicy mix until well coated. Drain well and season. Leave to cool.

3 Wipe out the wok with kitchen towels, heat it, then add the remaining oil. When the oil is hot, add the almonds and sprinkle in the sugar. Stir-fry gently until the almonds are golden brown and the sugar is caramelized. Place the cumin and salt in a bowl. Add the almonds, toss well, then leave to cool.

4 Mix the cashews, almonds and coconut flakes together, garnish with mustard and cress and serve with drinks.

Butterfly Prawns

Use raw prawns if you can because the flavour will be better, but if you substitute cooked prawns, cut down the stir-fry cooking time by one third.

Serves 4

INGREDIENTS
2.5 cm/1 in piece root ginger
350 g/12 oz raw prawns, thawed if frozen
50 g/2 oz/½ cup raw peanuts, roughly chopped
45 ml/3 tbsp vegetable oil
1 clove garlic, crushed
1 red chilli, finely chopped
45 ml/3 tbsp smooth peanut butter
15 ml/1 tbsp fresh coriander, chopped
fresh coriander sprigs, to garnish

FOR THE DRESSING
150 ml/¼ pint/⅔ cup natural low-fat yogurt
5 cm/2 in piece cucumber, diced
salt and freshly ground black pepper

diced cucumber

peanuts

prawn

coriander

chilli

1 To make the dressing, mix together the yogurt, cucumber and seasoning in a bowl, then leave to chill while preparing and cooking the prawns.

2 Peel the ginger, and chop it finely.

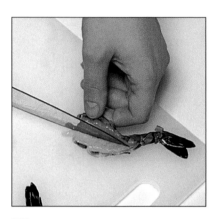

3 Prepare the prawns by peeling off the shells, leaving the tails intact. Make a slit down the back of each prawn and remove the black vein, then slit the prawn completely down the back and open it out to make a 'butterfly'.

4 Heat the wok and dry-fry the peanuts, stirring constantly until golden brown. Leave to cool. Wipe out the wok with kitchen towels.

5 Heat the wok, add the oil and when hot add the ginger, garlic and chilli. Stir-fry for 2–3 minutes until the garlic is softened but not brown.

6 Add the prawns, then increase the heat and stir-fry for 1–2 minutes until the prawns turn pink. Stir in the peanut butter and stir-fry for 2 minutes. Add the chopped coriander, then scatter in the peanuts. Garnish with coriander sprigs and serve with the cucumber dressing.

Swiss Rosemary Rosti

This traditional Swiss dish makes the perfect winter warmer. Serve it for breakfast, or as an unusual starter.

Serves 4

INGREDIENTS
350 g/12 oz cooked potatoes
45 ml/3 tbsp olive oil
10 ml/2 tsp fresh rosemary, chopped
pinch of freshly grated nutmeg
75 g/3 oz smoked bacon, cut
    into cubes
4 quail's eggs
salt flakes and freshly ground
    black pepper
fresh rosemary sprigs, to garnish

rosemary

smoked bacon

quail's eggs

potato

1 Coarsely grate the potatoes and thoroughly pat dry on kitchen towels to remove all the moisture.

2 Heat the wok, then add 30 ml/2 tbsp of oil. When the oil is hot, add the potatoes and cook them in batches until crisp and golden. This will take about 10 minutes. Drain them on kitchen towels, mix with the rosemary, nutmeg and seasoning and keep warm.

3 Add the bacon to the hot wok and stir-fry until crisp. Sprinkle the bacon on top of the potato, then season well.

4 Heat the wok, then add the remaining oil. When the oil is hot, fry the quail's eggs for about 2 minutes. Make a pile of the rosemary rosti, season it well, garnish with sprigs of fresh rosemary, then serve with the eggs.

Spicy Crab and Coconut

This spicy dish is delicious served with plain warm Naan bread.

Serves 4

INGREDIENTS

40 g/1½ oz dried unsweetened
    coconut flakes
2 cloves garlic
5 cm/2 in piece root ginger,
    peeled and grated
2.5 ml/½ tsp cumin seeds
1 small stick cinnamon
2.5 ml/½ tsp ground turmeric
2 dried red chillies
15 ml/1 tbsp coriander seeds
2.5 ml/½ tsp poppy seeds
15 ml/1 tbsp vegetable oil
1 medium onion, sliced
1 small green pepper, cut into strips
16 crab claws
fresh coriander sprigs, crushed,
to garnish
150 ml/¼ pint/⅔ cup natural low-fat
    yogurt, to serve

pepper

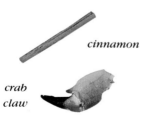

cumin seeds

cinnamon

crab claw

1 Place the dried coconut, garlic, ginger, cumin seeds, cinnamon, turmeric, red chillies, coriander and poppy seeds into a food processor and process until well blended.

2 Heat the oil in the wok and fry the onion until soft, but not coloured.

3 Stir in the green pepper and stir-fry for 1 minute.

4 Remove the vegetables with a slotted spoon and heat the wok. Add the crab claws, stir-fry for 2 minutes, then briefly return all the spiced vegetables to the wok. Garnish with fresh coriander sprigs and serve with the cooling yogurt.

Salmon Teriyaki

Marinating the salmon makes it so wonderfully tender, it just melts in the mouth, and the crunchy condiment provides an excellent foil. If you are short of time, you can buy good ready-made teriyaki sauce in a bottle.

Serves 4

INGREDIENTS
675 g/1½ lb salmon fillet
5 ml/1 tsp salt
30 ml/2 tbsp sunflower oil
watercress, to garnish

FOR THE TERIYAKI SAUCE
5 ml/1 tsp caster sugar
5 ml/1 tsp dry white wine
5 ml/1 tsp rice wine or dry sherry
30 ml/2 tbsp dark soy sauce

FOR THE CONDIMENT
5 cm/2 in piece root ginger, peeled
    and grated
few drops of pink food colouring
50 g/2 oz mooli, grated

salmon

watercress

soy sauce

ginger

mooli

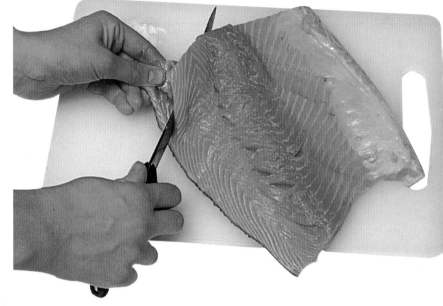

1 Mix all the teriyaki sauce ingredients together until the sugar dissolves.

2 To remove the skin from the salmon, sprinkle the salt over the chopping board to prevent the fish slipping, then use a very sharp fish filleting knife.

3 Cut the fillet into strips, then place it in a non-metallic dish. Pour the teriyaki sauce over the fish and leave to marinate for 10–15 minutes.

4 To make the condiment, place the ginger in a bowl, mix in the food colouring, then stir in the mooli.

5 Lift the salmon from the teriyaki sauce and drain.

6 Heat the wok, then add the oil. When the oil is hot, add the salmon and stir-fry in batches for 3–4 minutes until the fish is cooked. Garnish with watercress and serve with the mooli and ginger condiment.

Stir-fried Squid with Black Bean Sauce

If you cannot buy fresh squid you will find small or baby frozen squid, ready skinned, boned and with heads removed, at your local Oriental supermarket.

Serves 4

INGREDIENTS
1 large or 2 medium-sized squid
1 red chilli
10 ml/2 tsp peanut oil
1 clove garlic, crushed
30 ml/2 tbsp black bean sauce
60 ml/4 tbsp water
fresh parsley sprigs, to garnish
steamed rice, to serve

black bean sauce

garlic

squid

chillies

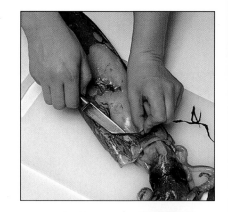

1 Carefully remove the skin from the squid and discard.

2 Cut off the head of each squid just below the eye, and discard.

3 Remove the bone from the squid and discard.

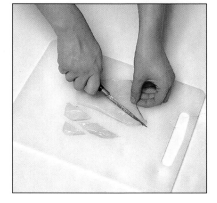

4 Cut the squid into bite-size pieces and score the flesh in a criss-cross pattern with a sharp knife.

5 Carefully deseed the chilli and chop it finely. Wear rubber gloves to protect your hands if necessary.

6 Heat the wok, then add the oil. When the oil is hot, add the garlic and cook until it starts to sizzle but does not colour. Stir in the squid and fry until the flesh starts to stiffen and turn white. Quickly stir in the black bean sauce, water and chilli. Continue stirring until the squid is cooked and tender (not more than a minute). Garnish with parsley sprigs and the tentacles and serve with steamed rice.

Fragrant Swordfish with Ginger and Lemon Grass

Swordfish is a meaty fish which cooks well in a wok if it has been marinated as a steak rather than in strips. If you cannot get swordfish, use tuna.

Serves 4

INGREDIENTS

1 kaffir lime leaf
45 ml/3 tbsp rock salt
75 ml/5 tbsp brown sugar
4 swordfish steaks, about
   225 g/8 oz each
1 stalk lemon grass, sliced
2.5 cm/1 in piece root ginger, cut into
   matchsticks
1 lime
15 ml/1 tbsp grapeseed oil
1 large ripe avocado, peeled and
   stoned
salt and freshly ground black pepper

avocado

ginger

lemon grass

lime

lime leaf

swordfish steak

1 Bruise the lime leaf by crushing slightly, to release the flavour.

2 To make the marinade, process the rock salt, brown sugar and lime leaf together in a food processor until thoroughly blended.

3 Place the swordfish steaks in a bowl. Sprinkle the marinade over them and add the lemon grass and ginger. Leave for 3–4 hours to marinate.

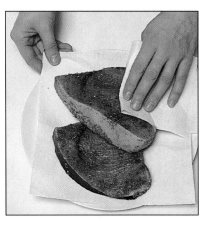

4 Rinse off the marinade and pat dry with kitchen towels.

5 Peel the lime. Remove any excess pith from the peel, then cut into very thin strips.

6 Heat the wok, then add the oil. When the oil is hot, add the lime rind and then the steaks, and stir-fry for 3–4 minutes. Add the juice of the lime. Remove from the heat, slice the avocado and add to the fish. Season and serve.

Sea Bass with Chinese Chives

Chinese chives are widely available in Oriental supermarkets but if you are unable to buy them, use half a large Spanish onion, finely sliced, instead.

Serves 4

INGREDIENTS
4 sea bass fillets, about 450 g/1 lb in all
5 ml/1 tsp cornflour
45 ml/3 tbsp vegetable oil
175 g/6 oz Chinese chives
15 ml/1 tbsp rice wine
5 ml/1 tsp caster sugar
salt and freshly ground pepper
Chinese chives with flowerheads,
    to garnish

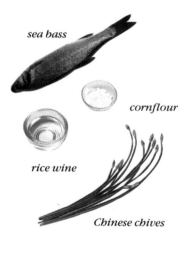

sea bass

cornflour

rice wine

Chinese chives

1 Remove the scales from the bass by scraping the fillets with the back of a knife, working from tail end to head end.

2 Cut the fillets into large chunks and dust them lightly with cornflour, salt and pepper.

3 Heat the wok, then add 30 ml/2 tbsp of the oil. When the oil is hot, toss the chunks of fish in the wok briefly to seal, then set aside. Wipe out the wok with kitchen towels.

4 Cut the Chinese chives into 5 cm/2 in lengths and discard the flowers. Heat the wok and add the remaining oil, then stir-fry the Chinese chives for 30 seconds. Add the fish and rice wine, then bring to the boil and stir in the sugar. Serve hot, garnished with some flowering Chinese chives, and with a side dish of crisp mixed lettuce salad.

Thai Fish Stir-fry

This is a substantial dish: it is best served with chunks of fresh crusty white bread, for mopping up all the delicious, spicy juices.

Serves 4

INGREDIENTS
675 g/1½ lb mixed seafood (for
    example, red snapper, cod, raw
    prawn tails) filleted and skinned
300 ml/½ pint/1¼ cups coconut milk
15 ml/1 tbsp vegetable oil
salt and freshly ground black pepper

FOR THE SAUCE
2 large red chillies
1 onion, roughly chopped
5 cm/2 in piece root ginger, peeled
    and sliced
5 cm/2 in piece lemon grass, outer leaf
    discarded, roughly sliced
5 cm/2 in piece galingale, peeled
    and sliced
6 blanched almonds, chopped
2.5 ml/½ tsp turmeric
2.5 ml/½ tsp salt

chilli

onion

ginger

prawn

1 Cut the filleted fish into large chunks. Peel the prawns, keeping their tails intact.

2 Carefully remove the seeds from the chillies and chop roughly, wearing rubber gloves to protect your hands if necessary. Then, make the sauce by putting the chillies and the other sauce ingredients in the food processor with 45 ml/3 tbsp of the coconut milk. Blend until smooth.

3 Heat the wok, then add the oil. When the oil is hot, stir-fry the seafood for 2–3 minutes, then remove.

4 Add the sauce and the remaining coconut milk to the wok, then return the seafood. Bring to the boil, season well and serve with crusty bread.

Oriental Scallops with Ginger Relish

Buy scallops in their shells to be absolutely sure of their freshness; your fishmonger will open them for you if you find this difficult. Remember to ask for the shells, which make excellent serving dishes.

Serves 4

INGREDIENTS
8 king or queen scallops
4 whole star anise
25 g/1 oz/2 tbsp unsalted butter
salt and freshly ground white pepper
fresh chervil sprigs and whole star
   anise, to garnish

FOR THE RELISH
½ cucumber, peeled
salt, for sprinkling
5 cm/2 in piece root ginger, peeled
10 ml/2 tsp caster sugar
45 ml/3 tbsp rice wine vinegar
10 ml/2 tsp ginger juice, strained from
   a jar of stem ginger
sesame seeds, for sprinkling

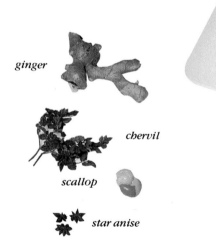

ginger

chervil

scallop

star anise

1 To make the relish, halve the cucumber lengthways and scoop out the seeds with a teaspoon.

2 Cut the cucumber into 2.5 cm/1 in pieces, place in a colander and sprinkle liberally with salt. Set aside for 30 minutes.

3 To prepare the scallops, cut each into 2–3 slices. Coarsely grind the star anise in a pestle and mortar.

4 Place the scallop slices with the corals in a bowl and marinate with the star anise and seasoning for about 1 hour.

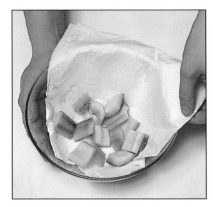

5 Rinse the cucumber under cold water and pat dry on kitchen towels. Cut the ginger into thin julienne strips and mix with the remaining relish ingredients. Cover and chill until needed.

6 Heat the wok and add the butter. When the butter is hot, add the scallop slices and stir-fry for 2–3 minutes. Garnish with sprigs of chervil and whole star anise, and serve with the cucumber relish, sprinkled with sesame seeds.

Pan-fried Red Mullet with Lemon

This spectacularly attractive and delicious dish is well worth the time it takes to prepare.

Serves 4

INGREDIENTS
1 large bulb fennel
1 lemon
12 red mullet fillets, skin left intact
45 ml/3 tbsp fresh marjoram, chopped
45 ml/3 tbsp olive oil
225 g/8 oz lamb's lettuce
salt and freshly ground black pepper

FOR THE VINAIGRETTE
200 ml/7 fl oz/generous ¾ cup
    peanut oil
15 ml/1 tbsp white wine vinegar
15 ml/1 tbsp sherry vinegar
salt and freshly ground black pepper

FOR THE SAUCE
40 g/1½ oz black olives
15 g/½ oz/1 tbsp unsalted butter
25 g/1 oz/1 tbsp capers

fennel

red mullet

marjoram

lamb's lettuce

1 Trim the fennel bulb and cut it into fine matchsticks. Peel the lemon. Remove any excess pith from the peel, then cut it into fine strips. Blanch the rind and refresh it immediately in cold water. Drain.

2 Make the vinaigrette by placing all the ingredients in a small bowl and lightly whisking until well mixed.

3 Sprinkle the red mullet fillets with salt, pepper and marjoram.

4 Heat the wok and add the olive oil. When the oil is very hot, add the fennel and stir-fry for 1 minute, then drain and remove.

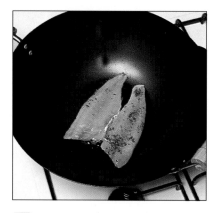

5 Reheat the wok and, when the oil is hot, stir-fry the red mullet fillets, cooking them skin-side down first for 2 minutes, then flipping them over for 1 further minute. Drain well on kitchen towels and wipe the wok clean with kitchen towels.

6 For the sauce, cut the olives into slivers. Heat the wok and add the butter. When the butter is hot, stir-fry the capers and olives for 1 minute. Toss the lamb's lettuce in the dressing. Arrange the fillets on a bed of lettuce, topped with the fennel and lemon, and serve with the olive and caper sauce.

Spiced Salmon Stir-fry

Marinating the salmon allows all the flavours to develop, and the lime tenderizes the fish beautifully, so it needs very little stir-frying – be careful not to overcook it.

Serves 4

INGREDIENTS
4 salmon steaks, about
   225 g/8 oz each
4 whole star anise
2 stalks lemon grass, sliced
juice of 3 limes
rind of 3 limes, finely grated
30 ml/2 tbsp clear honey
30 ml/2 tbsp grapeseed oil
salt and freshly ground black pepper
lime wedges, to garnish

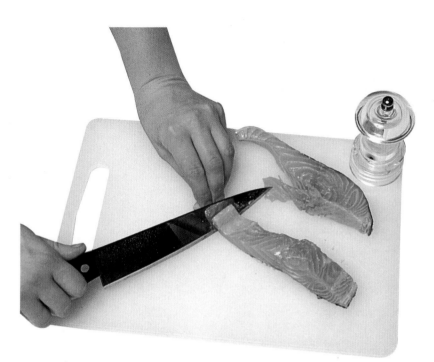

star anise

lime

lemon grass

clear honey

salmon steak

COOK'S TIP

Always dry off any marinade from meat, fish or vegetables to ensure that the hot oil does not splutter when you add them to the wok.

1 Remove the middle bone from each steak, using a very sharp filleting knife, to make two strips from each steak.

2 Remove the skin by inserting the knife at the thin end of each piece of salmon. Sprinkle 5 ml/1 tsp salt on the cutting board to prevent the fish slipping while removing the skin. Slice into pieces using diagonal cuts.

3 Coarsely crush the star anise in a pestle and mortar. Marinate the salmon in a non-metallic dish, with the star anise, lemon grass, lime juice and rind and honey. Season well with salt and pepper, cover and chill overnight.

4 Carefully drain the salmon from the marinade, pat dry on kitchen towels, and reserve the marinade.

5 Heat the wok, then add the oil. When the oil is hot, add the salmon and stir-fry, stirring constantly until cooked. Increase the heat, pour over the marinade and bring to the boil. Garnish with lime wedges and serve.

Chicken Liver Stir-fry

The final sprinkling of lemon, parsley and garlic gives this dish a delightful fresh flavour and wonderful aroma.

Serves 4

INGREDIENTS
500 g/1¼ lb chicken livers
75 g/3 oz/6 tbsp butter
175 g/6 oz field mushrooms
50 g/2 oz chanterelle mushrooms
3 cloves garlic, finely chopped
2 shallots, finely chopped
150 ml/¼ pint/⅔ cup medium sherry
3 fresh rosemary sprigs
30 ml/2 tbsp fresh parsley, chopped
rind of 1 lemon, grated
salt and freshly ground pepper
fresh rosemary sprigs, to garnish
4 thick slices of white toast, to serve

1 Clean and trim the chicken livers to remove any gristle or muscle.

2 Season the livers generously with salt and freshly ground black pepper, tossing well to coat thoroughly.

chanterelle mushrooms

field mushroom

lemon

rosemary

3 Heat the wok and add 15 g/½ oz/ 1 tbsp of the butter. When melted, add the livers in batches (melting more butter where necessary but reserving 25 g/1 oz/ 2 tbsp for the vegetables) and flash-fry until golden brown. Drain with a slotted spoon and transfer to a plate, then place in a low oven to keep warm.

4 Cut the field mushrooms into thick slices and, depending on the size of the chanterelles, cut in half.

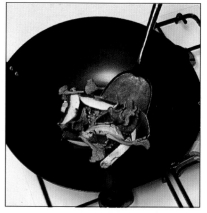

5 Heat the wok and add the remaining butter. When melted, stir in two-thirds of the chopped garlic and the shallots and stir-fry for 1 minute until golden brown. Stir in the mushrooms and continue to cook for a further 2 minutes.

6 Add the sherry, bring to the boil and simmer for 2–3 minutes until syrupy. Add the rosemary, salt and pepper and return livers to the pan. Stir-fry for 1 minute. Garnish with extra sprigs of rosemary, and serve sprinkled with a mixture of lemon, parsley and the remaining chopped garlic, with slices of toast.

Turkey with Sage, Prunes and Brandy

This stir-fry has a very rich sauce based on a good brandy – use the best you can afford.

Serves 4

INGREDIENTS

115 g/4 oz prunes
1.5 kg/3–3½ lb turkey breast
300 ml/½ pint/1¼ cups cognac
   or brandy
15 ml/1 tbsp fresh sage, chopped
150 g/5 oz smoked bacon, in
   one piece
50 g/2 oz/4 tbsp butter
24 baby onions, peeled and quartered
salt and freshly ground black pepper
fresh sage sprigs, to garnish

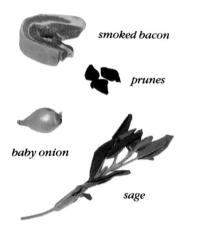

smoked bacon

prunes

baby onion

sage

1 Stone the prunes and cut them into slivers. Remove the skin from the turkey and cut the breast into thin pieces.

2 Mix together the prunes, turkey, cognac and sage in a non-metallic dish. Cover and leave to marinate overnight.

3 Next day, strain the turkey and prunes, reserving the cognac mixture, and pat dry on kitchen towels.

4 Cut the bacon into lardons (dice).

5 Heat the wok and add half the butter. When melted, add the onions and stir-fry for 4 minutes until crisp and golden. Set aside.

6 Heat the wok, add the lardons and stir-fry for 1 minute until the bacon begins to release some fat. Add the remaining butter and stir-fry the turkey and prunes for 3–4 minutes until crisp and golden. Push the turkey mixture to one side in the wok, add the cognac and simmer until thickened. Stir the turkey into the sauce, season well with salt and ground black pepper, and serve garnished with sage.

Spiced Honey Chicken Wings

Be prepared to get very sticky when you eat these wings, as the best way to enjoy them is by eating them with your fingers. Provide individual finger bowls for your guests.

Serves 4

INGREDIENTS
1 red chilli, finely chopped
5 ml/1 tsp chilli powder
5 ml/1 tsp ground ginger
rind of 1 lime, finely grated
12 chicken wings
60 ml/4 tbsp sunflower oil
15 ml/1 tbsp fresh coriander, chopped
30 ml/2 tbsp soy sauce
50 ml/3½ tbsp clear honey
lime rind and fresh coriander sprigs,
    to garnish

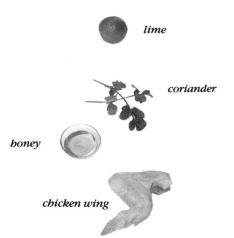

lime

coriander

honey

chicken wing

1 Mix the fresh chilli, chilli powder, ground ginger and lime rind together. Rub the mixture into the chicken skins and leave for at least 2 hours to allow the flavours to penetrate.

2 Heat the wok and add half of the oil. When the oil is hot, add half the wings and stir-fry for 10 minutes, turning regularly until crisp and golden. Drain on kitchen towels. Repeat with the remaining wings.

3 Add the coriander to the hot wok and stir-fry for 30 seconds, then return the wings to the wok and stir-fry for 1 minute.

4 Stir in the soy sauce and honey, and stir-fry for 1 minute. Serve the chicken wings hot with the sauce drizzled over them, garnished with lime rind and coriander sprigs.

Stir-fried Duck with Blueberries

Serve this conveniently quick dinner party dish with sprigs of fresh mint, which will give a wonderful fresh aroma as you bring the meal to the table.

Serves 4

INGREDIENTS
2 duck breasts, about 175 g/6 oz each
30 ml/2 tbsp sunflower oil
15 ml/1 tbsp red wine vinegar
5 ml/1 tsp sugar
5 ml/1 tsp red wine
5 ml/1 tsp *crème de cassis*
115 g/4 oz fresh blueberries
15 ml/1 tbsp fresh mint, chopped
salt and freshly ground black pepper
fresh mint sprigs, to garnish

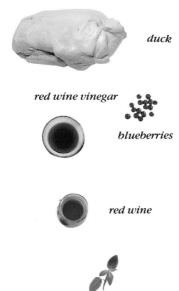

duck

red wine vinegar

blueberries

red wine

mint

1 Cut the duck breasts into neat slices. Season well with salt and pepper.

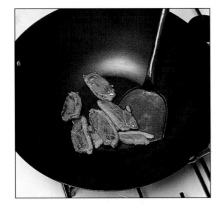

2 Heat the wok, then add the oil. When the oil is hot, stir-fry the duck for 3 minutes.

3 Add the red wine vinegar, sugar, red wine and *crème de cassis*. Bubble for 3 minutes, to reduce to a thick syrup.

4 Stir in the blueberries, sprinkle over the mint and serve garnished with sprigs of fresh mint.

Indonesian-style Satay Chicken

Use boneless chicken thighs to give a good flavour to these satays.

Serves 4

INGREDIENTS

50 g/2 oz/½ cup raw peanuts
45 ml/3 tbsp vegetable oil
1 small onion, finely chopped
2.5 cm/1 in piece root ginger, peeled
   and finely chopped
1 clove garlic, crushed
675 g/1½ lb chicken thighs, skinned
   and cut into cubes
90 g/3½ oz creamed coconut,
   roughly chopped
15 ml/1 tbsp chilli sauce
60 ml/4 tbsp crunchy peanut butter
5 ml/1 tsp soft dark brown sugar
150 ml/¼ pint/⅔ cup milk
1.2 ml/¼ tsp salt

creamed coconut

peanuts

chilli sauce

peanut butter

1 Shell and rub the skins from the peanuts, then soak them in enough water to cover, for 1 minute. Drain the nuts and cut them into slivers.

2 Heat the wok and add 5 ml/1 tsp oil. When the oil is hot, stir-fry the peanuts for 1 minute until crisp and golden. Remove with a slotted spoon and drain on kitchen towels.

3 Add the remaining oil to the hot wok. When the oil is hot, add the onion, ginger and garlic and stir-fry for 2–3 minutes until softened but not browned. Remove with a slotted spoon and drain on kitchen towels.

COOK'S TIP

Soak bamboo skewers in cold water for at least 2 hours, or preferably overnight, so they do not char when keeping the threaded chicken warm in the oven.

4 Add the chicken pieces and stir-fry for 3–4 minutes until crisp and golden on all sides. Thread on to pre-soaked bamboo skewers and keep warm.

5 Add the creamed coconut to the hot wok in small pieces and stir-fry until melted. Add the chilli sauce, peanut butter and cooked ginger and garlic, and simmer for 2 minutes. Stir in the sugar, milk and salt, and simmer for a further 3 minutes. Serve the skewered chicken hot, with a dish of the hot dipping sauce sprinkled with the roasted peanuts.

Duck and Ginger Chop Suey

Chicken can also be used in this recipe, but duck gives a richer contrast of flavours.

Serves 4

INGREDIENTS
2 duck breasts, about 175 g/6 oz each
45 ml/3 tbsp sunflower oil
1 × size 4 egg, lightly beaten
1 clove garlic
175 g/6 oz beansprouts
2 slices root ginger, cut into
   matchsticks
10 ml/2 tsp oyster sauce
2 spring onions, cut into matchsticks
salt and freshly ground pepper

FOR THE MARINADE
15 ml/1 tbsp clear honey
10 ml/2 tsp rice wine
10 ml/2 tsp light soy sauce
10 ml/2 tsp dark soy sauce

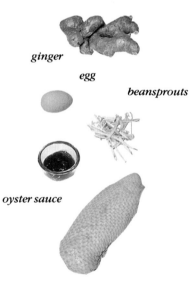

ginger

egg

beansprouts

oyster sauce

duck breast

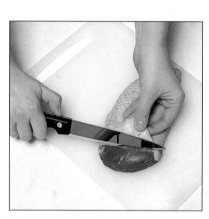

1 Remove the fat from the duck, cut the breasts into thin strips and place in a bowl. Mix the marinade ingredients together, pour over the duck, cover, chill and marinate overnight.

2 Next day, make the egg omelette. Heat a small frying pan and add 15 ml/1 tbsp of the oil. When the oil is hot, pour in the egg and swirl around to make an omelette. Once cooked, leave it to cool and cut into strips. Drain the duck and discard the marinade.

3 Bruise the garlic with the flat blade of a knife. Heat the wok, then add 10 ml/2 tsp oil. When the oil is hot, add the garlic and fry for 30 seconds, pressing it to release the flavour. Discard. Add the beansprouts with seasoning and stir-fry for 30 seconds. Transfer to a heated dish, draining off any liquid.

4 Heat the wok and add the remaining oil. When the oil is hot, stir-fry the duck for 3 minutes until cooked. Add the ginger and oyster sauce and stir-fry for a further 2 minutes. Add the beansprouts, egg strips and spring onions, stir-fry briefly and serve.

Chicken Teriyaki

A bowl of boiled rice is the ideal accompaniment to this Japanese-style chicken dish.

Serves 4

INGREDIENTS
450 g/1 lb boneless, skinless
    chicken breasts
orange segments and mustard and
    cress, to garnish

FOR THE MARINADE
5 ml/1 tsp sugar
15 ml/1 tbsp rice wine
15 ml/1 tbsp dry sherry
30 ml/2 tbsp dark soy sauce
rind of 1 orange, grated

orange

rice wine

soy sauce

chicken breast

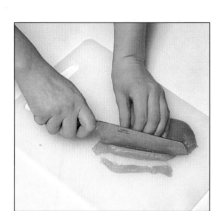

1 Finely slice the chicken.

2 Mix all the marinade ingredients together in a bowl.

COOK'S TIP
Make sure the marinade is brought to the boil and cooked for 4–5 minutes, because it has been in contact with raw chicken.

3 Place the chicken in a bowl, pour over the marinade and leave to marinate for 15 minutes.

4 Heat the wok, add the chicken and marinade and stir-fry for 4–5 minutes. Serve garnished with orange segments and mustard and cress.

Warm Stir-fried Salad

Warm salads are becoming increasingly popular because they are delicious and nutritious. Arrange the salad leaves on four individual plates, so the hot stir-fry can be served quickly on to them, ensuring the lettuce remains crisp and the chicken warm.

Serves 4

INGREDIENTS

15 ml/1 tbsp fresh tarragon
2 boneless, skinless chicken breasts, about 225 g/8 oz each
5 cm/2 in piece root ginger, peeled and finely chopped
45 ml/3 tbsp light soy sauce
15 ml/1 tbsp sugar
15 ml/1 tbsp sunflower oil
1 Chinese lettuce
½ frisée lettuce, torn into bite-size pieces
115 g/4 oz/cup unsalted cashews
2 large carrots, peeled and cut into fine strips
salt and freshly ground black pepper

chicken breast

carrot

ginger

cashews

1 Chop the tarragon.

2 Cut the chicken into fine strips and place in a bowl.

3 To make the marinade, mix together in a bowl the tarragon, ginger, soy sauce, sugar and seasoning.

4 Pour the marinade over the chicken strips and leave for 2–4 hours.

5 Strain the chicken from the marinade. Heat the wok, then add the oil. When the oil is hot, stir-fry the chicken for 3 minutes, add the marinade and bubble for 2–3 minutes.

6 Slice the Chinese lettuce and arrange on a plate with the frisée. Toss the cashews and carrots together with the chicken, pile on top of the bed of lettuce and serve immediately.

Sukiyaki-style Beef

This Japanese dish is a meal in itself; the recipe incorporates all the traditional elements – meat, vegetables, noodles and beancurd. If you want to do it all properly, eat the meal with chopsticks, and a spoon to collect the stock juices.

Serves 4

INGREDIENTS
450 g/1 lb thick rump steak
200 g/7 oz Japanese rice noodles
15 ml/1 tbsp shredded suet
200 g/7 oz hard beancurd, cut
    into cubes
8 shitake mushrooms, trimmed
2 medium leeks, sliced into 2.5 cm/
    1 in lengths
90 g/3½ oz baby spinach, to serve

FOR THE STOCK
15 ml/1 tbsp caster sugar
90 ml/6 tbsp rice wine
45 ml/3 tbsp dark soy sauce
125 ml/4 fl oz/½ cup water

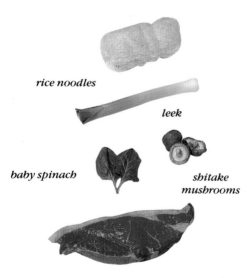

rice noodles

leek

baby spinach

shitake mushrooms

rump steak

1 Cut the beef into thin slices.

2 Blanch the noodles in boiling water for 2 minutes. Strain well.

3 Mix together all the stock ingredients in a bowl.

4 Heat the wok, then add the suet. When the suet is melted, stir-fry the beef for 2–3 minutes until it is cooked, but still pink in colour.

5 Pour the stock over the beef.

6 Add the remaining ingredients and cook for 4 minutes, until the leeks are tender. Serve a selection of the different ingredients, with a few baby spinach leaves, to each person.

Minted Lamb

Ask your butcher to remove the bone from a leg of lamb – it is sometimes called a butterfly leg of lamb – so that the meat can be sliced easily.

Serves 4

INGREDIENTS
450 g/1 lb boneless leg of lamb
30 ml/2 tbsp fresh mint, chopped
½ lemon
300 ml/½ pint/1¼ cups natural low-
    fat yogurt
15 ml/1 tbsp sunflower oil
salt and freshly ground black pepper
lemon wedges and fresh mint sprigs,
    to garnish

lemon

sunflower oil

mint

1 Using a sharp knife, cut the lamb into 6 mm/¼-in thick slices. Place in a bowl.

2 Sprinkle half the mint over the lamb, season well with salt and pepper and leave for 20 minutes.

3 Roughly cut up the lemon and place in the food processor. Process until finely chopped. Empty it into a bowl, then stir in the yogurt and remaining mint.

4 Heat the wok, then add the oil. When the oil is hot, add the lamb and stir-fry for 4–5 minutes until cooked. Serve with the yogurt dressing, garnished with a lemon wedge and fresh mint sprigs.

Oriental Beef

This sumptuously rich beef melts in the mouth, and is perfectly complemented by the cool, crunchy relish.

Serves 4

INGREDIENTS
450 g/1 lb rump steak

FOR THE MARINADE
15 ml/1 tbsp sunflower oil
2 cloves garlic, crushed
60 ml/4 tbsp dark soy sauce
30 ml/2 tbsp dry sherry
10 ml/2 tsp soft dark brown sugar

FOR THE RELISH
6 radishes
10 cm/4 in piece cucumber
1 piece stem ginger
4 whole radishes, to garnish

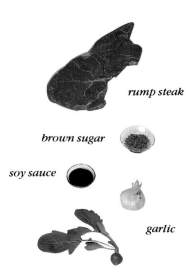

rump steak

brown sugar

soy sauce

garlic

radish

1 Cut the beef into thin strips. Place in a bowl.

2 To make the marinade, mix together the garlic, soy sauce, sherry and sugar in a bowl. Pour it over the beef and leave to marinate overnight.

3 To make the relish, chop the radishes and cucumber into matchsticks and the ginger into small matchsticks. Mix well together in a bowl.

4 Heat the wok, then add the oil. When the oil is hot, add the meat and marinade and stir-fry for 3–4 minutes. Serve with the relish, and garnish with a whole radish on each plate.

Stir-fried Pork with Mustard

Fry the apples for this dish very carefully, because they will disintegrate if they are overcooked.

Serves 4

INGREDIENTS
500 g/1¼ lb pork fillet
1 tart apple, such as Granny Smith
40 g/1½ oz/3 tbsp unsalted butter
15 ml/1 tbsp caster sugar
1 small onion, finely chopped
30 ml/2 tbsp Calvados or
    other brandy
15 ml/1 tbsp Meaux or coarse-grain
    mustard
150 ml/¼ pint/⅔ cup double cream
30 ml/2 tbsp fresh parsley, chopped
salt and freshly ground black pepper
flat-leaf parsley sprigs, to garnish

pork fillet

onion

mustard

apple

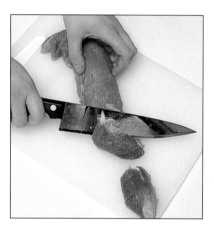

1 Cut the pork fillet into thin slices.

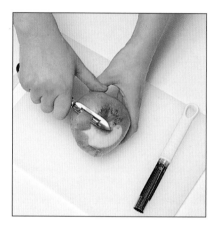

2 Peel and core the apple. Cut it into thick slices.

3 Heat the wok, then add half the butter. When the butter is hot, add the apple slices, sprinkle over the sugar, and stir-fry for 2–3 minutes. Remove the apple and set aside. Wipe out the wok with kitchen towels.

4 Heat the wok, then add the remaining butter and stir-fry the pork fillet and onion together for 2–3 minutes, until the pork is golden and the onion has begun to soften.

5 Stir in the Calvados or other brandy and boil until it is reduced by half. Stir in the mustard.

6 Add the cream and simmer for about 1 minute, then stir in the parsley. Serve garnished with sprigs of flat-leaf parsley.

Stir-fried Pork with Lychees

Lychees have a very pretty pink skin which, when peeled, reveals a soft fleshy berry with a hard shiny stone. If you cannot buy fresh lychees, this dish can be made with drained canned lychees.

Serves 4

INGREDIENTS
450 g/1 lb fatty pork, for example belly pork
30 ml/2 tbsp hoisin sauce
4 spring onions, sliced
175 g/6 oz lychees, peeled, stoned and cut into slivers
salt and freshly ground black pepper
fresh lychees and fresh parsley sprigs, to garnish

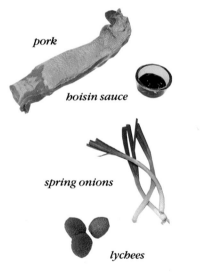

pork

hoisin sauce

spring onions

lychees

1 Cut the pork into bite-size pieces.

2 Pour the hoisin sauce over the pork and marinate for 30 minutes.

3 Heat the wok, then add the pork and stir-fry for 5 minutes until crisp and golden. Add the spring onions and stir-fry for a further 2 minutes.

4 Scatter the lychee slivers over the pork, and season well with salt and pepper. Garnish with fresh lychees and fresh parsley, and serve.

Glazed Lamb

Lemon and honey make a classically good combination in sweet dishes, and this lamb recipe shows how well they work together in savoury dishes, too. Serve with a fresh mixed salad to complete this delicious dish.

Serves 4

INGREDIENTS

450 g/1 lb boneless lean lamb
15 ml/1 tbsp grapeseed oil
175 g/6 oz mangetout peas, topped and tailed
3 spring onions, sliced
30 ml/2 tbsp clear honey
juice of half a lemon
30 ml/2 tbsp fresh coriander, chopped
15 ml/1 tbsp sesame seeds
salt and freshly ground black pepper

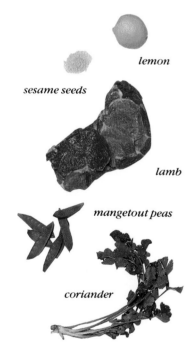

lemon

sesame seeds

lamb

mangetout peas

coriander

1 Using a sharp knife, cut the lamb into thin strips.

2 Heat the wok, then add the oil. When the oil is hot, stir-fry the lamb until browned all over. Remove from the wok and keep warm.

3 Add the mangetout peas and spring onions to the hot wok and stir-fry for 30 seconds.

4 Return the lamb to the wok and add the honey, lemon juice, coriander and sesame seeds, and season well. Bring to the boil and bubble for 1 minute until the lamb is well coated in the honey mixture.

Sizzling Beef with Celeriac Straw

The crisp celeriac matchsticks look like fine pieces of straw when cooked and have a mild celery-like flavour that is quite delicious.

Serves 4

INGREDIENTS
450 g/1 lb celeriac
150 ml/¼ pint/⅔ cup vegetable oil
1 red pepper
6 spring onions
450 g/1 lb rump steak
60 ml/4 tbsp beef stock
30 ml/2 tbsp sherry vinegar
10 ml/2 tsp Worcestershire sauce
10 ml/2 tsp tomato purée
salt and freshly ground black pepper

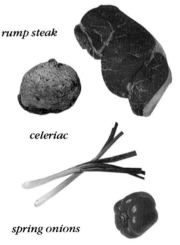

rump steak

celeriac

spring onions

pepper

1 Peel the celeriac and then cut it into fine matchsticks, using a cleaver.

2 Heat the wok, then add two-thirds of the oil. When the oil is hot, fry the celeriac matchsticks in batches until golden brown and crispy. Drain well on kitchen towels.

3 Chop the red pepper and the spring onions into 2.5 cm/1 in lengths, using diagonal cuts.

4 Chop the beef into strips, across the grain of the meat.

5 Heat the wok, and then add the remaining oil. When the oil is hot, stir-fry the chopped spring onions and red pepper for 2–3 minutes.

6 Add the beef strips and stir-fry for a further 3–4 minutes until well browned. Add the stock, vinegar, Worcestershire sauce and tomato purée. Season well and serve with the celeriac straw.

Veal Escalopes with Artichokes

Artichokes are very hard to prepare fresh, so use canned artichoke hearts, instead – they have an excellent flavour and are simple to use.

Serves 4

INGREDIENTS
450 g/1 lb veal escalopes
1 shallot
115 g/4 oz smoked bacon,
   finely chopped
1 × 400 g/14 oz can of artichoke
   hearts in brine, drained and
   quartered
150 ml/¼ pint/⅔ cup veal stock
3 fresh rosemary sprigs
60 ml/4 tbsp double cream
salt and freshly ground black pepper
fresh rosemary sprigs, to garnish

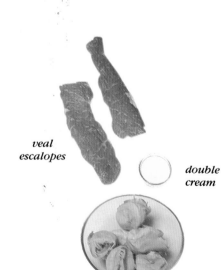

veal escalopes

double cream

artichoke hearts

I Cut the veal into thin slices.

2 Using a sharp knife, cut the shallot into thin slices.

3 Heat the wok, then add the bacon. Stir-fry for 2 minutes. When the fat is released, add the veal and shallot and stir-fry for 3–4 minutes.

4 Add the artichokes and stir-fry for 1 minute. Stir in the stock and rosemary and simmer for 2 minutes. Stir in the double cream, season with salt and pepper and serve garnished with sprigs of fresh rosemary.

Stir-fried Parsnips

Serve these sweet and piquant parsnips as an accompaniment to roast beef or as a vegetarian starter for two.

Serves 4 as an accompaniment

INGREDIENTS
2 large cloves garlic
350 g/12 oz parsnips
15 ml/1 tbsp vegetable oil
2.5 cm/1 in piece root ginger, peeled and grated
rind of 1 lime, grated
45 ml/3 tbsp clear honey
salt and freshly ground black pepper

lime

ginger

garlic

parsnip

1 Peel and cut the garlic into slices.

2 Peel and cut the parsnips into long, thin strands.

3 Heat the wok, then swirl in the oil. When the oil is hot, stir-fry the parsnips for 2 minutes.

4 Sprinkle the ginger, lime rind, salt and pepper and honey over the parsnips. Stir to coat the vegetables and serve.

Mooli, Beetroot and Carrot Stir-fry

This is a dazzling colourful dish with a crunchy texture and fragrant taste.

Serves 4 as an accompaniment

INGREDIENTS
25 g/1 oz/¼ cup pine nuts
115 g/4 oz mooli, peeled
115 g/4 oz raw beetroot, peeled
115 g/4 oz carrots, peeled
20 ml/1½ tbsp vegetable oil
juice of 1 orange
30 ml/2 tbsp fresh coriander, chopped
salt and freshly ground black pepper

pine nuts

carrot

mooli

beetroot

1 Heat the wok, then add the pine nuts and toss until golden brown. Remove and set aside.

2 Cut the mooli, beetroot and carrots into long thin strips.

3 Heat the wok and add one-third of the oil. When the oil is hot, stir-fry the mooli, beetroot and carrots for 2–3 minutes. Remove and set aside.

4 Pour the orange juice into the wok and simmer for 2 minutes. Remove and keep warm.

5 Arrange the vegetables in bundles, and sprinkle over the coriander and salt and pepper.

6 Drizzle over the orange juice, sprinkle in the pine nuts, and serve.

Pok Choi and Mushroom Stir-fry

Try to buy all the varieties of mushroom for this dish; the wild oyster and shitake mushrooms have particularly distinctive, delicate flavours.

Serves 4 as an accompaniment

INGREDIENTS
4 dried black Chinese mushrooms
450 g/1 lb pok choi
50 g/2 oz oyster mushrooms
50 g/2 oz shitake mushrooms
15 ml/1 tbsp vegetable oil
1 clove garlic, crushed
30 ml/2 tbsp oyster sauce

Chinese mushrooms

shitake mushrooms

pok choi

oyster mushrooms

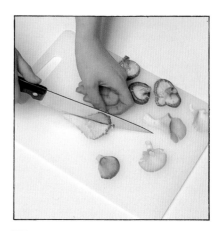

1 Soak the black Chinese mushrooms in 150 ml/¼ pint/⅔ cup boiling water for 15 minutes to soften.

2 Tear the pok choi into bite-size pieces with your fingers.

3 Halve any large oyster or shitake mushrooms, using a sharp knife.

4 Strain the Chinese mushrooms. Heat the wok, then add the oil. When the oil is hot, stir-fry the garlic until softened but not coloured.

5 Add the pok choi and stir-fry for 1 minute. Mix in all the mushrooms and stir-fry for 1 minute.

6 Add the oyster sauce, toss well and serve immediately.

Mixed Roasted Vegetables

Frying Parmesan cheese in this unusual way gives a wonderful crusty coating to the vegetables and creates a truly Mediterranean flavour.

Serves 4 as an accompaniment

INGREDIENTS
1 large aubergine, about 225 g/8 oz
salt, for sprinkling
175 g/6 oz plum tomatoes
2 red peppers
1 yellow pepper
30 ml/2 tbsp olive oil
25 g/1 oz Parmesan cheese
30 ml/2 tbsp fresh parsley, chopped
freshly ground black pepper

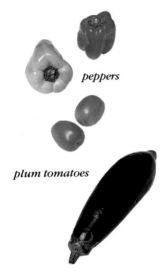

peppers

plum tomatoes

aubergine

1 Cut the aubergine into segments lengthwise. Place in a colander and sprinkle with salt. Leave for 30 minutes, to allow the salt to draw out the bitter juices.

2 Rinse off the salt under cold water and pat dry on kitchen towels.

3 Cut the plum tomatoes into segments lengthwise.

4 Cut the red and yellow peppers into quarters lengthwise and deseed.

5 Heat the wok, then add 5 ml/1 tsp of the olive oil. When the oil is hot, add the Parmesan and stir-fry until golden brown. Remove from the wok, allow to cool and chop into fine flakes.

6 Heat the wok, and then add the remaining oil. When the oil is hot stir-fry the aubergine and peppers for 4–5 minutes. Stir in the tomatoes and stir-fry for a further 1 minute. Toss the vegetables in the Parmesan, parsley and black pepper and serve.

Stir-fried Chickpeas

Buy canned chickpeas and you will save all the time needed for soaking and then thoroughly cooking dried chickpeas. Served with a crisp green salad, this dish makes a filling vegetarian main course for two, or could be served in smaller quantities as a starter.

Serves 2–4 as an accompaniment

INGREDIENTS

30 ml/2 tbsp sunflower seeds
1 × 400 g/14 oz can chickpeas,
   drained
5 ml/1 tsp chilli powder
5 ml/1 tsp paprika
30 ml/2 tbsp vegetable oil
1 clove garlic, crushed
200 g/7 oz canned chopped tomatoes
225 g/8 oz fresh spinach, coarse
   stalks removed
salt and freshly ground black pepper
10 ml/2 tsp chilli oil

spinach

garlic

sunflower seeds

chickpeas

1 Heat the wok, and then add the sunflower seeds. Dry-fry until the seeds are golden and toasted.

2 Remove the sunflower seeds and set aside. Toss the chickpeas in chilli powder and paprika. Remove and reserve.

3 Heat the wok, then add the oil. When the oil is hot, stir-fry the garlic for 30 seconds, add the chickpeas and stir-fry for 1 minute.

4 Stir in the tomatoes and stir-fry for 4 minutes. Toss in the spinach, season well and stir-fry for 1 minute. Drizzle chilli oil and scatter sunflower seeds over the vegetables, then serve.

Marinated Mixed Vegetables with Basil Oil

Basil oil is a must for drizzling over plain stir-fried vegetables. Once it has been made up, it will keep in the fridge for up to 2 weeks.

Serves 2–4 as an accompaniment

INGREDIENTS

15 ml/1 tbsp olive oil
1 clove garlic, crushed
rind of 1 lemon, finely grated
1 × 400 g/14 oz can artichoke hearts, drained
2 large leeks, sliced
225 g/8 oz patty pan squash, halved if large
115 g/4 oz plum tomatoes, cut into segments lengthwise
15 g/½ oz basil leaves
150 ml/¼ pint/⅔ cup olive oil
salt and freshly ground black pepper

patty pan squash

artichoke hearts

leek

plum tomatoes

1 Mix together the olive oil, garlic and lemon rind in a bowl, to make a marinade.

2 Place the artichokes, leeks, patty pan squash and plum tomatoes in a large bowl, pour over the marinade and leave for 30 minutes.

3 Meanwhile, make the basil oil. Blend the basil leaves with the extra-virgin olive oil in a food processor until puréed.

4 Heat the wok, then stir-fry the marinated vegetables for 3–4 minutes, tossing well. Drizzle the basil oil over the vegetables and serve.

Spiced Vegetables with Coconut

This spicy and substantial dish could be served as a starter, or as a vegetarian main course for two. Eat it with spoons and forks, and hunks of granary bread for mopping up the delicious coconut milk.

Serves 2–4 as a starter

INGREDIENTS
1 red chilli
2 large carrots
6 stalks celery
1 bulb fennel
30 ml/2 tbsp grapeseed oil
2.5 cm/1 in piece root ginger, peeled and grated
1 clove garlic, crushed
3 spring onions, sliced
1 × 400 ml/14 fl oz can thin coconut milk
15 ml/1 tbsp fresh coriander, chopped
salt and freshly ground black pepper
coriander sprigs, to garnish

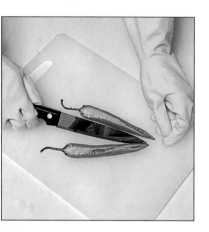

celery

spring onions

fennel

carrot

1 Halve, deseed and finely chop the chilli. If necessary, wear rubber gloves to protect your hands.

2 Slice the carrots on the diagonal. Slice the celery stalks on the diagonal.

3 Trim the fennel head and slice roughly, using a sharp knife.

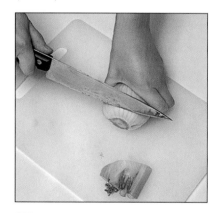

4 Heat the wok, then add the oil. When the oil is hot, add the ginger and garlic, chilli, carrots, celery, fennel and spring onions and stir-fry for 2 minutes.

5 Stir in the coconut milk with a large spoon and bring to the boil.

6 Stir in the coriander and salt and pepper, and serve garnished with coriander sprigs.

Spicy Vegetable Fritters with Thai Salsa

The Thai salsa goes just as well with plain stir-fried salmon strips or stir-fried beef as it does with these courgette fritters.

Serves 2–4 as a starter

INGREDIENTS
10 ml/2 tsp cumin seeds
10 ml/2 tsp coriander seeds
450 g/1 lb courgettes
115 g/4 oz/1 cup chickpea (gram) flour
2.5 ml/½ tsp bicarbonate of soda
125 ml/4 fl oz/½ cup groundnut oil
fresh mint sprigs, to garnish

FOR THE THAI SALSA
½ cucumber, diced
3 spring onions, chopped
6 radishes, cubed
30 ml/2 tbsp fresh mint, chopped
2.5 cm/1 in piece root ginger, peeled and grated
45 ml/3 tbsp lime juice
30 ml/2 tbsp caster sugar
3 cloves garlic, crushed

cucumber

mint　*ginger*

radishes

courgette

1 Heat the wok, then toast the cumin and coriander seeds. Cool them, then grind well, using a pestle and mortar.

2 Cut the courgettes into 7.5 cm/3 in sticks. Place in a bowl.

3 Blend the flour, bicarbonate of soda, spices and salt and pepper in a food processor. Add 125 ml/4 fl oz warm water with 15 ml/1 tbsp groundnut oil, and blend again.

4 Coat the courgettes in the batter, then leave to stand for 10 minutes.

5 To make the Thai salsa, mix all the ingredients together in a bowl.

6 Heat the wok, then add the remaining oil. When the oil is hot, stir-fry the courgettes in batches. Drain well on kitchen towels, then serve hot with the salsa, garnished with fresh mint sprigs.

Beancurd Stir-fry

The beancurd has a pleasant creamy texture, which contrasts well with crunchy stir-fried vegetables. Make sure you buy firm beancurd which is easy to cut neatly.

Serves 2–4

INGREDIENTS
115 g/4 oz hard white cabbage
2 green chillies
225 g/8 oz firm beancurd
45 ml/3 tbsp vegetable oil
2 cloves garlic, crushed
3 spring onions, chopped
175 g/6 oz French beans, topped
  and tailed
175 g/6 oz baby sweetcorn, halved
115 g/4 oz beansprouts
45 ml/3 tbsp smooth peanut butter
20 ml/1½ tbsp dark soy sauce
300 ml/½ pint/1¼ cups coconut milk

baby sweetcorn

beansprouts

chilli

beancurd

French beans

1 Shred the white cabbage. Carefully remove the seeds from the chillies and chop finely. Wear rubber gloves to protect your hands, if necessary.

2 Cut the beancurd into strips.

3 Heat the wok, then add 30 ml/2 tbsp of the oil. When the oil is hot, add the beancurd, stir-fry for 3 minutes and remove. Set aside. Wipe out the wok with kitchen towels.

4 Add the remaining oil. When it is hot, add the garlic, onions and chillies and stir-fry for 1 minute. Add the French beans, sweetcorn and beansprouts and stir-fry for a further 2 minutes.

5 Add the peanut butter and soy sauce. Stir well to coat the vegetables. Add the beancurd to the vegetables.

6 Pour the coconut milk over the vegetables, simmer for 3 minutes and serve immediately.

Crispy Cabbage

This makes a wonderful accompaniment to meat or vegetable dishes – just a couple of spoonfuls will add crispy texture to a meal. It goes especially well with prawn dishes.

Serves 2–4 as an accompaniment

INGREDIENTS
4 juniper berries
1 large Savoy cabbage
60 ml/4 tbsp vegetable oil
1 clove garlic, crushed
5 ml/1 tsp caster sugar
5 ml/1 tsp salt

cabbage

vegetable oil

garlic

juniper berries

1 Finely crush the juniper berries, using a pestle and mortar.

2 Finely shred the cabbage.

3 Heat the wok, then add the oil. When the oil is hot, stir-fry the garlic for 1 minute. Add the cabbage and stir-fry for 3–4 minutes until crispy. Remove and pat dry with kitchen towels.

4 Return the cabbage to the wok. Toss the cabbage in sugar, salt and crushed juniper berries and serve hot or cold.

Oriental Vegetable Noodles

Thin Italian egg pasta is a good alternative to Oriental egg noodles; use it fresh or dried.

Serves 6

INGREDIENTS
500 g/1¼ lb thin tagliarini
1 red onion
115 g/4 oz shitake mushrooms
45 ml/3 tbsp sesame oil
45 ml/3 tbsp dark soy sauce
15 ml/1 tbsp balsamic vinegar
10 ml/2 tsp caster sugar
5 ml/1 tsp salt
celery leaves, to garnish

tagliarini

shitake mushrooms

red onion

balsamic vinegar

soy sauce

1 Boil the tagliarini in a large pan of salted boiling water, following the instructions on the pack.

2 Thinly slice the red onion and the mushrooms, using a sharp knife.

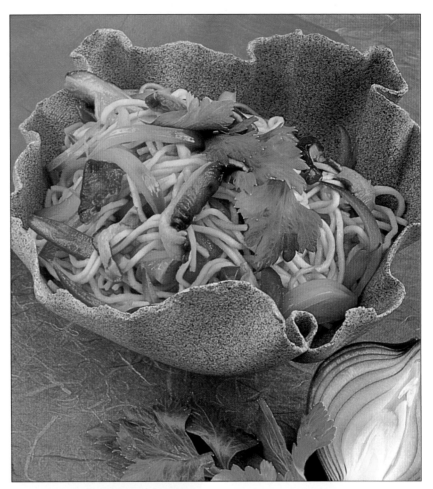

3 Heat the wok, then add 15 ml/1 tbsp of the sesame oil. When the oil is hot, stir-fry the onion and mushrooms for 2 minutes.

4 Drain the tagliarini, then add to the wok with the soy sauce, balsamic vinegar, sugar and salt. Stir-fry for 1 minute, then add the remaining sesame oil, and serve garnished with celery leaves.

Fried Singapore Noodles

Thai fish cakes vary in their size, and their hotness. You can buy them from Oriental supermarkets, but, if you cannot get hold of them, simply omit them from the recipe.

Serves 4

INGREDIENTS
175 g/6 oz rice noodles
60 ml/4 tbsp vegetable oil
2.5 ml/½ tsp salt
75 g/3 oz cooked prawns
175 g/6 oz cooked pork, cut
  into matchsticks
1 green pepper, seeded and chopped
  into matchsticks
2.5 ml/½ tsp sugar
10 ml/2 tsp curry powder
75 g/3 oz Thai fish cakes
10 ml/2 tsp dark soy sauce

rice noodles

pork

pepper

prawns

1 Soak the rice noodles in water for about 10 minutes, drain well, then pat dry with kitchen towels.

2 Heat the wok, then add half the oil. When the oil is hot, add the noodles and salt and stir-fry for 2 minutes. Transfer to a heated serving dish to keep warm.

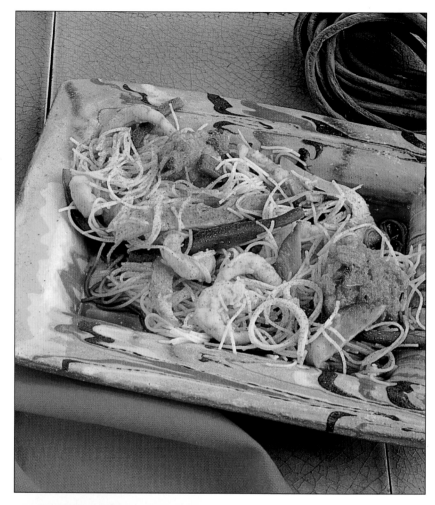

3 Heat the remaining oil and add the prawns, pork, pepper, sugar, curry powder and remaining salt. Stir-fry the ingredients for 1 minute.

4 Return the noodles to the pan and stir-fry with the Thai fish cakes for 2 minutes. Stir in the soy sauce and serve.

Mixed Rice Noodles

A delicious noodle dish made extra special by adding avocado and garnishing with prawns.

Serves 4

INGREDIENTS
15 ml/1 tbsp sunflower oil
2.5 cm/1 in piece root ginger, peeled
 and grated
2 cloves garlic, crushed
45 ml/3 tbsp dark soy sauce
225 g/8 oz peas, thawed if frozen
450 g/1 lb rice noodles
450 g/1 lb fresh spinach, coarse
 stalks removed
30 ml/2 tbsp smooth peanut butter
30 ml/2 tbsp tahini
150 ml/¼ pint/⅔ cup milk
1 ripe avocado, peeled and stoned
roasted peanuts and peeled prawns,
 to garnish

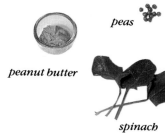

rice noodles

ginger

peas

peanut butter

spinach

1 Heat the wok, then add the oil. When the oil is hot, stir-fry the ginger and garlic for 30 seconds. Add 15 ml/1 tbsp of the soy sauce and 150 ml/¼ pint/⅔ cup boiling water.

2 Add the peas and noodles, then cook for 3 minutes. Stir in the spinach. Remove the vegetables and noodles, drain and keep warm.

3 Stir the peanut butter, remaining soy sauce, tahini and milk together in the wok, and simmer for 1 minute.

4 Add the vegetables and noodles, slice in the avocado and toss together. Serve piled on individual plates. Spoon some sauce over each portion and garnish with peanuts and prawns.

Nasi Goreng

This dish is originally from Thailand, but can easily be adapted by adding any cooked ingredients you have to hand. Crispy prawn crackers make an ideal accompaniment.

Serves 4

INGREDIENTS
225 g/8 oz long grain rice
2 × size 3 eggs
30 ml/2 tbsp vegetable oil
1 green chilli
2 spring onions, roughly chopped
2 cloves garlic, crushed
225 g/8 oz cooked chicken
225 g/8 oz cooked prawns
45 ml/3 tbsp dark soy sauce
prawn crackers, to serve

rice

soy sauce

egg

chilli

prawns

1 Rinse the rice and then cook for 10–12 minutes in 500 ml/1 pint water in a saucepan with a tight-fitting lid. When cooked, refresh under cold water.

2 Lightly beat the eggs. Heat 15 ml/ 1 tbsp of oil in a small frying pan and swirl in the beaten egg. When cooked on one side, flip over and cook on the other side, remove from the pan and leave to cool. Cut the omelette into strips.

3 Carefully remove the seeds from the chilli and chop finely, wearing rubber gloves to protect your hands if necessary. Place the spring onions, chilli and garlic in a food processor and blend to a paste.

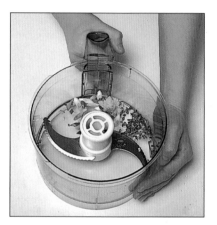

4 Heat the wok, and then add the remaining oil. When the oil is hot, add the paste and stir-fry for 1 minute.

5 Add the chicken and prawns.

6 Add the rice and stir-fry for 3–4 minutes. Stir in the soy sauce and serve with prawn crackers.

Chinese Jewelled Rice

This rice dish, with its many different, interesting ingredients, can make a meal in itself.

Serves 4

INGREDIENTS

350 g/12 oz long grain rice
45 ml/3 tbsp vegetable oil
1 onion, roughly chopped
115 g/4 oz cooked ham, diced
175 g/6 oz canned white crabmeat
75 g/3 oz canned water chestnuts,
  drained and cut into cubes
4 dried black Chinese mushrooms,
  soaked, drained and cut into dice
115 g/4 oz peas, thawed if frozen
30 ml/2 tbsp oyster sauce
5 ml/1 tsp sugar

rice

Chinese mushrooms

diced ham

water chestnuts

peas

crabmeat

1 Rinse the rice, then cook for 10–12 minutes in 700–850 ml/1 ¼–1 ½ pints water in a saucepan with a tight-fitting lid. When cooked, refresh under cold water. Heat the wok, then add half the oil. When the oil is hot, stir-fry the rice for 3 minutes, then remove and set aside.

2 Add the remaining oil to the wok. When the oil is hot, cook the onion until softened but not coloured.

3 Add all the remaining ingredients and stir-fry for 2 minutes.

4 Return the rice to the wok and stir-fry for 3 minutes, then serve.

Nutty Rice and Mushroom Stir-fry

This delicious and substantial supper dish can be eaten hot or cold with salads.

Serves 4–6

INGREDIENTS

350 g/12 oz long grain rice
45 ml/3 tbsp sunflower oil
1 small onion, roughly chopped
225 g/8 oz field mushrooms, sliced
50 g/2 oz/½ cup hazelnuts,
 roughly chopped
50 g/2 oz/½ cup pecan nuts,
 roughly chopped
50 g/2 oz/½ cup almonds,
 roughly chopped
60 ml/4 tbsp fresh parsley, chopped
salt and freshly ground black pepper

rice

almonds

field mushroom

hazelnuts

1 Rinse the rice, then cook for 10–12 minutes in 700–850 ml/1¼–1½ pints water in a saucepan with a tight-fitting lid. When cooked, refresh under cold water. Heat the wok, then add half the oil. When the oil is hot, stir-fry the rice for 2–3 minutes. Remove and set aside.

2 Add the remaining oil and stir-fry the onion for 2 minutes until softened.

3 Mix in the field mushrooms and stir-fry for 2 minutes.

4 Add all the nuts and stir-fry for 1 minute. Return the rice to the wok and stir-fry for 3 minutes. Season with salt and pepper. Stir in the parsley and serve.

Mee Krob

This delicious dish makes a filling meal. Take care when frying vermicelli as it has a tendency to spit when added to hot oil.

Serves 4

INGREDIENTS
125 ml/4 fl oz/½ cup vegetable oil
225 g/8 oz rice vermicelli
150 g/5 oz French beans, topped,
    tailed and halved lengthwise
1 onion, finely chopped
2 boneless, skinless chicken breasts,
    about 175 g/6 oz each, cut
    into strips
5 ml/1 tsp chilli powder
225 g/8 oz cooked prawns
45 ml/3 tbsp dark soy sauce
45 ml/3 tbsp white wine vinegar
10 ml/2 tsp caster sugar
fresh coriander sprigs, to garnish

chicken breast

rice vermicelli

onion

French beans

prawns

1 Heat the wok, then add 60 ml/4 tbsp of the oil. Break up the vermicelli into 7.5 cm/3 in lengths. When the oil is hot, fry the vermicelli in batches. Remove from the heat and keep warm.

2 Heat the remaining oil in the wok, then add the French beans, onion and chicken and stir-fry for 3 minutes until the chicken is cooked.

3 Sprinkle in the chilli powder. Stir in the prawns, soy sauce, vinegar and sugar, and stir-fry for 2 minutes.

4 Serve the chicken, prawns and vegetables on the vermicelli, garnished with sprigs of fresh coriander.

Crispy Cinnamon Toasts

This recipe is based on a sweet version of French toast. You can use fancy cutters to create a pretty dessert or, if you do not have cutters, simply cut the crusts off the bread and cut it into little fingers.

Serves 4

INGREDIENTS
50 g/2 oz raisins
45 ml/3 tbsp Grand Marnier
4 medium slices white bread
3 × size 4 eggs, beaten
15 ml/1 tbsp ground cinnamon
2 large oranges
20 ml/1½ tbsp sunflower oil
25 g/1 oz/2 tbsp unsalted butter
15 ml/1 tbsp demerara sugar
thick Greek yogurt, to serve

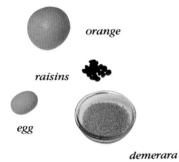
orange

raisins

egg

demerara

bread

1 Soak the raisins in the Grand Marnier for 10 minutes.

2 Cut the bread into shapes with a cutter. Place the shapes in a bowl with the eggs and cinnamon to soak.

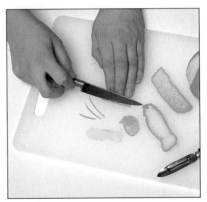

3 Peel the oranges. Remove any excess pith from the peel, then cut it into fine strips and blanch. Refresh it in cold water, then drain.

4 Strain the raisins. Heat the wok, then add the oil. When the oil is hot, stir in the butter until melted, then add the bread and fry, turning once, until golden brown. Stir in the raisins and orange rind, and sprinkle with sugar. Serve warm with thick Greek yogurt.

Mango and Coconut Stir-fry

Choose a ripe mango for this recipe. If you buy one that is a little under-ripe, leave it in a warm place for a day or two before using.

Serves 4

INGREDIENTS
¼ coconut
1 large, ripe mango
juice of 2 limes
rind of 2 limes, finely grated
15 ml/1 tbsp sunflower oil
15 g/½ oz/1 tbsp butter
30 ml/1½ tbsp clear honey
crème fraîche, to serve

coconut

mango

honey

lime

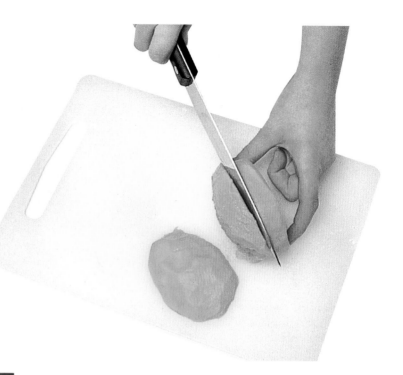

1 Prepare the coconut flakes by draining the milk from the coconut and peeling the flesh with a vegetable peeler.

2 Peel the mango. Cut the stone out of the middle of the fruit. Cut each half of the mango into slices.

3 Place the mango slices in a bowl and pour over the lime juice and rind, to marinate them.

4 Meanwhile, heat the wok, then add 10 ml/2 tsp of the oil. When the oil is hot, add the butter. When the butter has melted, stir in the coconut flakes and stir-fry for 1–2 minutes until the coconut is golden brown. Remove and drain on kitchen towels. Wipe out the wok. Strain the mango slices, reserving the juice.

5 Heat the wok and add the remaining oil. When the oil is hot, add the mango and stir-fry for 1–2 minutes, then add the juice and allow to bubble and reduce for 1 minute. Then stir in the honey, sprinkle on the coconut flakes and serve with crème fraîche.

COOK'S TIP

Because of the delicate taste of desserts, always make sure your wok has been scrupulously cleaned so there is no transference of flavours – a garlicky mango isn't quite the effect you want to achieve!

Caramelized Apples

A sweet, sticky dessert which is very quickly made, and usually very quickly eaten!

Serves 4

INGREDIENTS
675 g/1½ lb dessert apples
115 g/4 oz/½ cup unsalted butter
25 g/1 oz fresh white breadcrumbs
50 g/2 oz/½ cup ground almonds
rind of 2 lemons, finely grated
60 ml/4 tbsp golden syrup
60 ml/4 tbsp thick Greek yogurt,
    to serve

lemon

golden syrup

ground almonds

apple

1 Peel and core the apples.

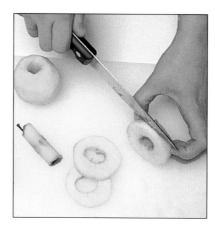

2 Carefully cut the apples into 1 cm/½ in-thick rings.

3 Heat the wok, then add the butter. When the butter has melted, add the apple rings and stir-fry for 4 minutes until golden and tender. Remove from the wok, reserving the butter. Add the breadcrumbs to the hot butter and stir-fry for 1 minute.

4 Stir in the ground almonds and lemon rind and stir-fry for a further 3 minutes, stirring constantly. Sprinkle the breadcrumb mix over the apples, then drizzle warmed golden syrup over the top. Serve with thick Greek yogurt.

INDEX

ACKNOWLEDGEMENTS

The author and publishers would like to thank Wing Yip, 395 Edgware Road, London NW2 for the loan of equipment for photography. Other branches can be found at 375 Nechells Park Road, Nechells, Birmingham, B7 5NT and Oldham Road, Manchester, M8 4BA.